DARING WOMEN

25
WOMEN
WHO
PROTECTED *Their* COUNTRY

by Emma Carlson Berne

COMPASS POINT BOOKS
a capstone imprint

Daring Women is published by Compass Point Books, an imprint of Capstone.
1710 Roe Crest Drive
North Mankato, Minnesota 56003
www.capstonepub.com

Library of Congress Cataloging-in-Publication Data is available on the Library of Congress website.
ISBN: 978-0-7565-6618-0 (hardcover)
ISBN: 978-0-7565-6662-3 (paperback)
ISBN: 978-0-7565-6626-5 (ebook PDF)

Summary: Discover 25 women who served their countries and accomplished great feats of strength and bravery. Whether through medicine, espionage, journalism, or combat, these 25 women show what it takes to be a hero.

Image Credits
Alamy: Archive PL, 31, GL Archive, 47, History collection 2016, 9, Jens Benninghofen, 50, PJF Military Collection, cover, 11, UtCon Collection, 53; AP Images: AP Photo, 26; Bridgeman Images: Prismatic Pictures, 54; DIVIDS: MNCI PAO/U.S. Army photo by Spc. Jeremy D. Crisp, 28, U.S. Army photos by Sgt. Nicholas T. Holmes, 14; Getty Images: Apic, 49, Bettmann, 12, 39, FPG/Archive Photos, 33, Gamma-Keystone, 51, John Stillwell - PA Images, 43, Patrick Durand, 21, Scott Peterson, 41, Theo Wargo, 45, United News/ Popperfoto, 35; Library of Congress Prints and Photographs Division: 7, 19, 27; Newscom: MOLLY RILEY/REUTERS, 24; Shutterstock Premier: Denis Cameron, 36; Shutterstock: Lutsenko_Oleksandr, 16, Vladimirs Koskins, 5; Wikimedia: NARA, 22, Public Domain, U.S. Army, 15, U.S. Army Official Photograph, 38
Design Elements by Shutterstock

Editorial Credits
Editor: Kristen Mohn; Designer: Bobbie Nuytten; Media Researcher: Tracy Cummins; Production Specialist: Laura Manthe

Printed in the United States of America.
PA117

TABLE OF CONTENTS

INTRODUCTION

Wars require incredible bravery. Soldiers, civilians, correspondents, medics, doctors, and nurses must be prepared to see horrific sights. They may save lives, take lives, or risk their own. Though much of history has focused on men's roles in war, women have been a part of warfare for as long as it has existed.

Alongside their male counterparts—and sometimes forging ahead—women have fired shots, flown fighter planes, phoned in news dispatches as bullets whizzed around them, and passed along critical, secret information. They have faced down prejudice and discrimination from those who believed women could not be calm, collected, and courageous under fire. Women who protect their country have been all of those things, proving their critics wrong.

> *I have had the opportunity to witness women soldiers jump out of airplanes, hike 10 miles, lead men and women, even under the toughest circumstances. . . . Thousands of women have been decorated for valor. . . . Today, what was once a band of brothers has truly become a band of brothers and sisters.*
> —Army General Ann E. Dunwoody, first female four-star general

When the United States ended its draft in 1973, women represented just 2 percent of enlisted forces. By 2018 that number was 16 percent.

Chapter 1

WORKING WITH THE WOUNDED

In groundbreaking military hospitals, in helicopters, and in bullet-ridden roadside ditches, women doctors, nurses, and combat medics have saved the lives of their own soldiers, and often, of those on the enemy side. They've taught themselves new medical techniques under pressure and stayed focused on their jobs while bombs were exploding around them. Their first concern was always on the wounded people who needed their help.

Edith Cavell
(1865–1915)

Born in 1865 in Norfolk, England, Cavell had a peaceful childhood with her sisters. She became a governess and later, after nursing her father through an illness, decided to become a nurse. This decision would lead her to save lives in more ways than one.

Cavell trained in England, then moved to Belgium to help found that country's first nursing school and training hospital. When World War I (1914–1918) broke out, the nursing school became a Red Cross hospital, and Cavell helped the wounded soldiers there.

Belgium, a British ally, was under German occupation. But Cavell ordered her nurses to treat any soldier who came

Edith Cavell, photographed shortly before her death

to the hospital, regardless of whose side they were on. In the fall of 1914, Cavell arranged for two wounded Allied soldiers at her hospital to be smuggled out to the neutral Netherlands, where they would be safe. From 1914 to 1915, Cavell smuggled out more than 200 Allied soldiers, using an underground tunnel.

Cavell often spoke out against the German occupation, and German authorities became suspicious of her. Despite the risk, Cavell refused to stop her underground smuggling. In summer 1915, a soldier who was collaborating with the Germans came through Cavell's hospital and betrayed her. On August 5, 1915, she was arrested by the German police and placed in a solitary prison cell.

On October 12, 1915, Cavell was executed by a German firing squad. Right before her execution, Cavell said, "I realize that patriotism is not enough. I must have no hatred or bitterness towards anyone."

The German authorities did not succeed in erasing what Cavell had done. Outrage over her death spread throughout the Allied countries, which considered her a martyr. In 1919, after the war was over, Cavell's body was brought back to England and a memorial service was held at Westminster Abbey. Thousands lined the streets in remembrance of her bravery.

Flora Murray
(1869–1923)

Flora Murray was a Scottish physician, a militant women's rights suffragist, and a medical pioneer. Together with her lifelong companion and fellow doctor Louisa Anderson, Murray cofounded the first World War I–era hospital staffed and run entirely by women.

Murray became a doctor during a time when female doctors were few and were trained only so that they could care for women and children. In 1912 Murray cofounded the Women's Hospital for Children in London. She was a suffragist

Dr. Flora Murray discharged patients at the Endell Street Military Hospital, 1915.

and an active member of a women's rights group. She used her medical training to treat suffragists who had been force-fed during hunger strikes and those who had been injured during marches.

As World War I began, the British medical system became overwhelmed by the horrific wounds caused by machine gun and artillery fire. Undaunted, Murray and Anderson formed the Women's Hospital Corps, which was made up entirely of suffragists. They established two military hospitals in France and then set up the Endell Street Military Hospital in London, also run entirely by women. Before the war, people tended to be prejudiced against female doctors. They didn't think they had the same skills as men. But now that doctors were desperately needed, people were more willing to accept women as physicians.

Murray and the other female nurses and physicians had no training in treating the massive combat wounds that flooded their hospital. They plunged in anyway, learning surgical techniques on the job. They were so skillful that some men refused to leave the hospital when their discharge came.

Endell Street was the longest-operating military hospital of the war, and Murray worked there until it closed in 1919. She, Anderson, and their staff showed the world that women medical teams could do the same work as men, advancing the cause of female doctors everywhere.

Jane Kendeigh
(1922–1987)

Born in 1922, U.S. Navy flight nurse Jane Kendeigh was the first nurse to work on an active Pacific battlefield in World War II (1939–1945). On March 6, 1945, Kendeigh was on board a hospital transport plane as it approached the island of Iwo Jima in the Pacific Ocean. So many shells were being fired on the island that the explosions looked like Fourth of July fireworks. Kendeigh was only 22, and she was scared.

But once the plane landed, Kendeigh remembers that she was too busy to be frightened anymore. The wounded lay in rows near the runways, and Kendeigh evaluated each one. She supervised the loading of the wounded onto the transport plane for the eight-hour evacuation flight to Guam.

A journalist who was on the same flight as Kendeigh remembers watching her work nonstop, administering medicine, changing bandages, and, in one case, using a tube to feed a soldier who had been shot in the neck. Though busy with her medical tasks, Kendeigh still found time to visit with and reassure the soldiers.

Kendeigh made multiple successful evacuation flights during the war and prided herself on never losing a patient

U.S. Navy flight nurse Jane Kendeigh, 1945

during a flight. Eventually, she and her fellow flight nurses helped safely move more than 2,000 wounded soldiers from the battlefield.

Kendeigh didn't want to stop. When the navy sent her to safety in the United States, she requested a transfer back to an active combat zone—this time on the island of Okinawa, Japan. On April 7, 1945, only six days after the United States had invaded Okinawa, Kendeigh was part of the first flight to land on the island. She had made history again.

President Dwight D. Eisenhower awarded the Medal of Freedom to Geneviève de Galard in 1954.

Geneviève de Galard
(1925–)

Geneviève de Galard was a teenager in France during World War II and lived through Nazi occupation. That time gave de Galard a fighting spirit. She decided to dedicate her life to nursing and, at age 18, became a flight nurse in the French Air Force. At the time, France was involved in an eight-year-long war in what was then called Indochina, which included the countries of Laos, Cambodia, and Vietnam. The war was reaching a critical point, and a battle began near a mountain outpost called Dien Bien Phu.

De Galard was never supposed to be on the battlefield. But on March 28, 1954, she was on a plane meant to evacuate the wounded French soldiers from Dien Bien Phu. Upon landing, the plane plowed through a barbed wire fence, which pierced the oil tank. The plane was grounded on an active battlefield with desperately wounded soldiers lying on stretchers nearby. They were trapped—and an easy target.

The only woman among 11,000 troops, de Galard swung into action, tending to the most severely wounded soldiers and moving the less injured under shelter. That night, their plane was hit by artillery fire and exploded.

For 10 days, de Galard nursed wounded men in a 40-bed underground bunker. She worked so hard and slept so little that she felt she was hallucinating. The conditions were horrific, dirty, and brutal. But she kept working. On April 29, the brigadier general at the outpost made de Galard a knight in the French Foreign Legion—France's highest military honor.

The French lost at Dien Bien Phu. De Galard was captured and held for 17 days by the Viet Minh, a group leading the effort for Vietnamese independence. De Galard was called "the Angel of Dien Bien Phu" for her actions and bravery. In July 1954, de Galard was invited to the United States. President Dwight D. Eisenhower awarded her the Medal of Freedom, honoring her inspiration to all those in the free world. He stated, "Her service to her comrades, marked by the courage of a woman in battle and by the devotion of a nurse to her sworn duty, has been unsurpassed in this century."

Nadja West

(1961–)

Nadja West, the first black female lieutenant general and surgeon general of the U.S. Army, was raised in a military family. Born in 1961, West was one of 12 adopted brothers and sisters, most of whom grew up to serve in the military. West's father, Oscar Grammer, served in the army for more than three decades. Army culture influenced everything the family did.

Even in high school, West knew she wanted army life. She joined ROTC (the Reserve Officer Training Corps) and then went to the elite military academy West Point. When West graduated in 1982, she was part of only the third class at West Point to include women.

West knew she liked science, and she knew she liked working with people. "Medicine is one of those places where you can have the best of both worlds," she said in an interview. She eventually attended George

Lieutenant General Nadja West was the 44th surgeon general of the United States Army.

Washington University to get her medical degree and became a dermatologist and family medicine doctor at an army hospital.

West was deployed during Operation Desert Storm and served as a captain and a medical officer. She tended to wounded soldiers on the battlefield. During her career, she also served as chief medical advisor at the Pentagon.

In 2015, West was named surgeon general of the U.S. Army. A surgeon general's job has two parts: the medical part and the military part. The surgeon general is the head of the health department of an armed services branch. West was the perfect fit.

As the army's surgeon general, West developed programs to help combat medics keep their skills sharp between deployments. And she focused on making sure that soldiers and their families at home were physically and emotionally ready to deploy when they were needed. West retired as surgeon general in August 2019, providing military women everywhere a proud legacy.

Monica Lin Brown in Afghanistan in 2008, during Operation Enduring Freedom

Monica Lin Brown
(1988–)

Army medic Monica Lin Brown grew up in central Texas and went to nine different schools because her family moved around frequently. Still, she was a brilliant student and graduated from high school at 17. When her older brother Justin stopped by an army recruiting office, Brown went along—and joined too. In 2005, she enlisted as a medic. In 2007, she was deployed to Afghanistan.

The conditions at Brown's base were primitive, but she loved it and thrived on the constant missions. On April 25, 2007, Brown was riding in a convoy of Humvees that had just turned into a dry streambed. One Humvee hit an improvised explosive device (IED) and burst into flames.

Brown grabbed her medic bag and scrambled out of her vehicle. The enemy was firing on the convoy and, along with another soldier, Brown ran through gunfire. She dragged the wounded soldiers into a ditch and flung herself on top, shielding them from bullets with her own body. Later, a comrade said he was shocked Brown hadn't been killed.

Brown and another soldier loaded the wounded onto a truck and rode with them. She bandaged the badly bleeding head of one soldier and held the hand of another who was burned and in shock. She never

Combat medics might carry some or all of the following items: tourniquets, large bandages, small bandages, gauze coated with medicine to stop bleeding, splints, a heat blanket, syringes, saline fluid, and heavy-duty scissors called medical shears.

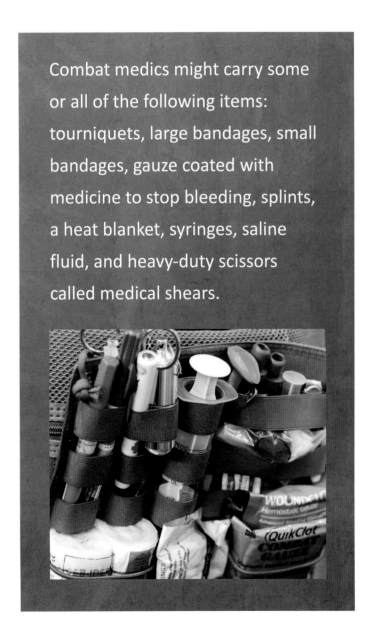

looked up from her job until the wounded were loaded onto an evacuation helicopter.

In March 2008, Brown was awarded the Silver Star for valor, the United States' third-highest combat medal. The army's statement read, "[Brown's] bravery, unselfish actions, and medical aid rendered under fire saved the lives of her comrades and represents the finest traditions of heroism in combat." Brown is only the second woman since World War II to receive that medal.

THE IMPACT OF IEDS

Many devastating injuries and deaths in the wars in Iraq and Afghanistan have been caused by improvised explosive devices. These small, homemade bombs are among the world's oldest types of weapons. They can be produced cheaply and easily and can be carried in a suitcase, mailed, tossed, or buried. In addition to explosive material, IEDs can be packed with shards of glass, nails, or pieces of metal. These sharp objects are shot toward a target with deadly force when the IED explodes. Between half and two-thirds of the Americans killed or wounded in the Iraq and Afghanistan wars have been victims of IEDs.

Chapter 2

BRAVERY ON THE BATTLEFIELD

For much of history, women were not permitted to fight in direct ground combat. But they fought nonetheless. In the U.S. military, they flew fighter planes, commanded squadrons and battalions, drove trucks with shells exploding around them, and patrolled outposts. In the United States, the last barrier for women has been lifted, and they are now permitted to fight in combat. These soldiers are walking the path laid by the women in combat around the world who came before them.

Maria Bochkareva
(1889–1920)

Maria Bochkareva did not seem destined for a life of success. She was born in Siberia, Russia, in 1889. Her alcoholic father beat her, her mother, and her sisters, and Bochkareva was married off to another violent alcoholic at age 15. In 1914, Germany declared war on Russia in what would soon become World War I. Bochkareva saw a way out. She petitioned the Russian leader, the czar, directly by telegram asking to join the Russian army.

Maria Bochkareva was the first Russian woman to command a military unit.

She got permission and entered its ranks.

Bochkareva loved military life—the barracks, the discipline, the uniforms. She was wounded twice and awarded medals for bravery three times. But by 1917, Russia was suffering terrible losses, despite fighting on the Allied side. In an attempt at propaganda, the government created the Russian Women's Battalion of Death, an all-female fighting battalion. Two thousand women applied; 300 were selected. Bochkareva was their commander.

But Bochkareva and her battalion were too late—Russia's losses were mounting even as Bochkareva was preparing. The attack they mounted was a failure, and the battalion was dissolved. Russia withdrew from the war. Bochkareva was almost executed and only narrowly escaped to the United States. She returned to Russia after a few years and tried to rejoin army life and reform the Women's Battalion. But Russia was now enmeshed in a civil war, and Bochkareva had joined the side that was losing—the anti-communist army. When the Communists captured her, they held and questioned her for four months. Then they sent her to the firing squad. Bochkareva was executed on May 16, 1920. She was 30 years old.

Susan Travers
(1909–2003)

Born in 1909 in London, England, Susan Travers was the only female soldier to serve in the French Foreign Legion—an elite branch of the Allied French army—during World War II. Travers grew up in the south of France playing tennis and going to parties as the daughter of a wealthy family. But when World War II erupted in Europe, Travers found her purpose in life—and what she considered her true family—in the Foreign Legion.

Travers was posted to Libya in 1942 as an army driver and was stationed at a desert camp called Bir Hakeim. In June of that year, the Allied forces began taking

Susan Travers was the only female to serve in the French Foreign Legion, an Allied military group with members from many countries.

at the camp, General Marie-Pierre Kœnig, should break out. And Travers would drive him.

That night, while driving through a minefield with shells exploding all around her and two top commanding officers as her passengers, Travers floored the accelerator of the army vehicle. With bullets piercing her car and gunfire filling the air, she drove straight through enemy lines, carving a path for other Allied vehicles to follow.

More than 2,000 Allied troops escaped the camp along with Travers and Kœnig. For her heroism, Travers was awarded the French medal of bravery, the *Croix de Guerre*—the War Cross. "I just happen to be a person who is not frightened. . . . I am not afraid," Travers said much later in her life. The Battle of Bir Hakeim was a crucial battle for France. Travers helped lead that victory.

intense enemy fire from Italian and German troops. The Allies were surrounded on all sides, running out of water, and broiling in extreme heat. The enemy was entrenched in three expanding rings around the camp. It was decided that the commanding officer

The French Foreign Legion allows foreign recruits who are willing to serve in the French military to join its ranks. Today, it has about 8,000 members from many countries.

Major Charity Adams Earley (in the dark uniform in front) inspected the 6888th Central Postal Directory Battalion in England, February 1945.

Charity Adams Earley
(1918–2002)

Born in 1918 and raised in Columbia, South Carolina, Charity Adams Earley would become the first African American woman to lead a unit of fellow soldiers overseas. Her parents valued education, and Earley was a brilliant student and valedictorian of her class. She won a scholarship to Wilberforce University, one of the top schools for African American students, who were not allowed to attend most universities at that time.

When the United States mobilized for World War II, Earley mobilized too. In 1942, she joined the Women's Army Auxiliary Corps, the women's branch of the U.S. Army. In 1944, she was promoted to major and was chosen to lead the first all–African American, all-female unit of soldiers to be deployed overseas.

The unit was sent to Birmingham, England, to sort mail. Earley and the other women in her unit were some of the first black people that Birmingham residents had ever met. Their job was to make sure the soldiers' mail came in and went out properly, but first they had to organize and clear a massive backlog—the air hangars full of mail. Directed by Earley, they worked around the clock in three shifts and cleared the backlog in three months, which was three months ahead of schedule.

Earley also had to contend with racism on a regular basis, but she fought back. When a commanding officer was visiting her battalion and threatened to send a white officer over to show her how to run the unit, Earley replied, "Over my dead body, sir." He threatened to court-martial her— the military equivalent of being arrested. Earley was not intimidated. She threatened to file charges against *him*.

Earley came home from the war to earn a master's degree and become a college dean. She gave many speeches about her war experiences and was listed by the national Smithsonian Institution in Washington, D.C., as one of the most historically important black women.

Linda McTague
(1957–2017)

Brigadier General Linda McTague at a task force meeting in early 2009 to discuss military support for President Barack Obama's inauguration

When Linda McTague joined the military in 1981, women still weren't allowed to fly in combat. Of course, women had been flying military aircraft since World War II, but those were support roles. McTague would see that change.

McTague was born in 1957 in Michigan and joined the air force after attending graduate school. By 1988, she was flying "operational support" airlift planes, airlifting soldiers when they needed help. In 1993, women were first allowed to fly combat planes. By then, McTague was a career U.S. Air Force officer. In 1997, she commanded a squadron that flew dignitaries and members of Congress around the world.

Over the years, McTague logged 5,250 flight hours and rose to the rank of brigadier general. She taught flying and parachuting at the U.S. Air Force Academy in Colorado Springs, Colorado. In 2003, McTague took command of the D.C. Air National Guard's 113th Wing, which includes an air force fighter squadron. She was the first woman in U.S. military history to take such a command.

Despite this, McTague insisted that she wasn't a pioneer. In 2009, she retired from the air force with many honors. She spent her time working with other military veterans and riding her beloved motorcycle. On May 10, 2017, McTague was killed in a motorcycle accident. In her life, she'd been true to the goal she'd always set for herself and those serving under her: to "not settle for being less than the best."

Linda Bray
(1960–)

Linda Bray just wanted to do her job. She didn't want to become the center of a national controversy. But that is what

happened. Born in 1960 in Sanford, North Carolina, Bray joined ROTC in 1982, then served as a military policewoman in Germany.

In 1989 Bray was commanding a company of military police during the United States' invasion of Panama. Military police are in charge of protecting bases and military outposts. They're the law enforcement arm of the military, and they are considered noncombatants. At the time, women were not supposed to participate in combat in the U.S. military.

But military police have assault teams too. That's what Bray was leading on December 20 when her team received orders to infiltrate a dog kennel held by the Panamanian Defense Forces. Bray and her team—nearly all men—broke into the kennel and exchanged gunfire with the enemy soldiers hiding inside. What they expected to be a 10-minute mission turned into a three-hour firefight. Most of the Panamanian soldiers fled, and Bray's

Linda Bray at an army base in Panama City, Panama, 1990

team found a cache of weapons and ammunition inside.

Bray had performed bravely and admirably, but she'd also become part of a controversy. Many felt that the mission had crossed the line between peacekeeping and offensive combat. For the very first time, U.S. troops had been led by a woman in combat. Bray came under intense scrutiny for what she had done.

WOMEN IN COMBAT

Women have always been a part of wars as nurses, caretakers, and defenders of their own homes and farms. But in the United States, it wasn't until World War II that women entered the military in great numbers. Women were on the front lines of that war—they were allowed to fly military planes, though they were not allowed to engage in combat.

In 1948, the Women's Armed Service Integration Act was signed into law, allowing women to become full-fledged, permanent members of the military in wartime and in peace. Before this, women were considered temporary members who were released from the military when the war was over. But women would have to wait more than 60 years after this act went into effect to be permitted to serve in direct ground combat.

1942 poster recruiting women for the U.S. Navy

Congresswoman Patricia Schroeder of Colorado called for an end to the ban on women in combat based on Bray's role. But the Pentagon did not agree. Many even questioned whether Bray had exaggerated her role in the conflict.

The experience left Bray frustrated with the military. In 1991, she asked to be discharged and entered civilian life. In 2013, the military's prohibition on women in ground combat was finally lifted. Bray was thrilled to learn that women would now be serving "right beside" men.

Leigh Ann Hester
(1982–)

Leigh Ann Hester was eager to join the military as soon as she could. She became a part of ROTC in high school. In 2001, motivated by the September 11 terrorist attacks, she enlisted in the Kentucky National Guard.

Just a few years later, while deployed

Sergeant Leigh Ann Hester was the first female to receive the Silver Star Medal for valor in combat.

in Iraq in 2004, Hester earned her place in history. She was guarding a convoy of trucks moving along a road near Baghdad. As a military police officer, she was in charge of scanning the terrain and detecting threats such as IEDs. This mission was routine for Hester. She'd done it many times before.

But today was different. Three miles into their trip, the truck in front of Hester's was hit with a rocket-propelled grenade. Then the convoy was bombarded with enemy bullets. Shouting orders to her squad, Hester threw two grenades at the enemy before jumping from her truck and running toward the enemy's position. She dropped into an irrigation ditch and started firing. Forty-five minutes later, the battle was over. Every member of her squad had survived.

For "combat valor"—bravery in combat—Hester received the Silver Star, the United States' third-highest combat medal. She was the first woman since World War II to receive the medal with that designation. But Hester doesn't see herself as a hero. "I was trained to do what I did, and I did it," she said in an interview.

Hester left the military in 2009 and became a police officer. But she missed military life and reenlisted in the National Guard in 2010. She served until 2017 and earned many medals and commendations— and inspired countless other women in the military.

> *I was trained to do what I did, and I did it.*
> –Leigh Ann Hester

Chapter 3

DISPATCHES FROM THE FRONT LINES

War correspondents take us to the battlefields with the pictures painted by their words. The women whose stories follow had a mandate: tell the truth. Their job was to observe horrors and bravery and provide an unbiased report back to the public. But they were also storytellers. They needed to capture the lives and actions of the people they saw around them and make those people come to life on the page. These brave journalists did that, at great risk to themselves, and our knowledge is richer because of their work.

Alice Askew
(1874–1917)

Alice Askew knew about horror. Born near Hyde Park, England, in 1874, she was a well-known horror and mystery author along with her husband, Claude Askew. Together, they wrote more than 90 books and created the supernatural detective character Aylmer Vance.

When World War I began, the Askews traveled to Serbia as correspondents for the British newspaper *Daily Express*. Stationed near a British field hospital, they

Alice Askew, author and journalist

were assigned to report on the battles and injuries they saw.

This time, their horror writing required no imagination. In their 1916 book about their experiences, *The Stricken Land: Serbia as We Saw It*, Alice and Claude wrote:

> *Words could hardly give adequate description of the horrors that prevailed . . . Every train discharged a pitiful cargo—the brave sons of Serbia who had been wounded on the battlefield—and though hospitals were rapidly improvised throughout the town, they were utterly insufficient to cope with the need. Medical necessities were lacking; doctors and nurses—the few that were available—worked themselves to death, literally to death, in their efforts to stem the horrid tide, but they were only drawn into the vortex themselves. Men died in the streets, for there were none to minister to them . . .*

Alice and Claude Askew died in 1917 when the Italian steamship they were traveling on was torpedoed by a German submarine. The steamer sank and the authors drowned. At a time when most women did not work outside the home, much less travel the world, visit war zones, and write for major newspapers, Alice Askew was a pioneer. She did not live to see the contributions of later female war correspondents—but she was there at the beginning.

Martha Gellhorn
(1908–1998)

Martha Gellhorn was the first female correspondent at D-Day in World War II, was present at the liberation of the Dachau concentration camp in Germany at the end of the war, and covered major conflicts around the world for six decades.

Born in St. Louis in 1908, Gellhorn was raised in an educated and forward-thinking family. After attending Bryn Mawr College,

Gellhorn went to work for *The New Republic* magazine in 1927 and also covered crime for a local newspaper. She found her way to Spain in 1937 with a backpack, $50, and nerves of steel. There, she started covering the Spanish Civil War for *Collier's* magazine. During World War II, she wrote about the Blitz as bombs fell on London. She stowed away on a ship during D-Day and snuck ashore by posing as a stretcher-bearer so she could write firsthand accounts. She wrote unflinchingly about the starving people at Dachau, forcing her readers to see the horrors alongside her.

Gellhorn reported honestly what was right in front of her. "You go into a hospital, and it's full of

War correspondent Martha Gellhorn believed in reporting from the field to provide readers accurate, firsthand accounts.

Martha Gellhorn was married to the famous author Ernest Hemingway from 1940 to 1945, but she disliked being identified with him after their divorce.

wounded kids," the *New York Times* quoted her as saying. "You write what you see and how it is." She firmly believed that a good war correspondent needed to be on the ground, talking with soldiers on the battlefield, not getting briefings from miles away.

After World War II, Gellhorn covered the Vietnam War, the Six-Day War in the Middle East, and conflicts in South America. Gellhorn continued reporting into her 80s and covered the United States' invasion of Panama at age 81. In 1998, at age 89, Gellhorn died of cancer at her home.

Clare Hollingworth
(1911–2017)

Clare Hollingworth was born into a wealthy and quiet life in England in 1911. When she was a teenager, her parents insisted she attend "domestic science" college to learn how to run a home. She was bored stiff. She announced to her parents that she was going to become a journalist. She left for eastern Europe, where she helped refugees and wrote about them. In August 1939, she was hired by the British newspaper *The Telegraph* to cover the rumblings of war happening at the Polish-German border.

On August 28, 1939, barely a week into her new job, Hollingworth commandeered an official car and was allowed through the German border by Nazi guards who believed she was a member of the British government. Driving along a road near the border, she saw a tarpaulin draped across the view of a nearby valley. The wind lifted the tarp, and Hollingworth saw tanks and troops massed there—waiting to invade Poland.

She drove as fast as she could back over the border to Poland and telephoned her editor. Her article came out the next day. She was the first reporter in the world to break the news of the start of World War II.

Clare Hollingworth was the first reporter to break the news of the start of World War II.

Over the many decades of her long career, Hollingworth never stopped reporting from hot spots and battlefields. She preferred to dress in a safari suit and often said that all she needed for happiness was a toothbrush, a typewriter, and a revolver. During her career she once slept buried up to her neck in desert sand for warmth and held off an angry police officer in Algeria by threatening to hit him with her shoe. Machine gun fire didn't scare her, she said. The excitement of the job overwhelmed the fear.

Hollingworth was still reporting into her 80s. Even into her 90s, she often slept on the floor of her bedroom to keep herself from getting "soft." She was living in Hong Kong when she died in 2017 at age 105.

*Gloria Emerson with photographer
Richard Avedon in Vietnam, 1972*

Gloria Emerson

(1929–2004)

Born in New York City to well-off but alcoholic parents, Gloria Emerson ran away from home after high school. She was hired by the *New York Times* in 1957 to write about women's fashion, a subject she hated but that provided a living. She was transferred by the *Times* to Paris in 1964 to cover fashion shows.

Emerson found the work irritating and trivial, and she began insisting the *Times* let her cover war. Finally, the paper sent her to write about the conflicts in Belfast, Northern Ireland, and Nigeria. When Emerson was sent to Vietnam in 1970, she believed it was because the war was nearly over—therefore, it didn't matter if a female correspondent went.

But Emerson wrote unflinchingly about the destruction and suffering that she saw, and she tried to make Americans see the Vietnamese as people just like them. She wanted to write about ordinary infantry soldiers and the South Vietnamese villagers whose country had been decimated.

Emerson often wrote whatever she wanted, despite the directions of her bureau chief. She could be bossy, possessive, and rude. But she never stopped feeling the suffering of others around her. While in Vietnam, she persuaded airline crews to smuggle in antibiotics that could be used to treat injured children.

In 1978, Emerson won the National Book Award for *Winners and Losers*, about the United States and the Vietnam War. For one year, in 1989, she lived on the Gaza Strip among citizens caught up in the fighting between the Israelis and the Palestinians.

In 1994, Emerson injured her leg and wasn't fully mobile anymore. But she kept writing, fiction as well as nonfiction, until Parkinson's disease made it hard for her to type—her greatest fear realized. Emerson died in New York in 2004 at age 75.

Kate Webb
(1943–2007)

Kate Webb was born in Christchurch, New Zealand. Her parents were killed in a car accident when she was 18, and she had to fend for herself after that.

When she wanted to report on Vietnam in 1967, she paid her own way and showed up with an old typewriter and a

REPORTING FROM THE FIELD

Kate Webb sent back a graphic, poetic report of a raid on the U.S. embassy by Vietcong guerrillas on January 31, 1968. She was one of the first journalists at the scene. Later, her report would become famous as an excellent piece of reporting history:

I moved behind a Marine closer to the embassy gates. I wanted to get the Marine's name, and home town. It seemed ridiculous to ask for it at this time. They called out, "There's a Marine dead on the roof up there," . . . "Get help over to that jeep," . . . "It's no good I tell you, they're dead," . . . "There's one guy sitting there, he's alive," . . . "He was my buddy."

At the white walled embassy, the green lawns and white ornamental fountains were strewn with bodies. The teak door was blasted. The weary defenders were pickaxing their way warily among the dead and around live rockets.

The Vietcong, or National Liberation Front, fought with the North Vietnamese army against the United States and South Vietnam governments during the Vietnam War.

couple hundred dollars. She started work as a freelancer for the United Press International (UPI), reporting on politics and eventually going out to the battlefield—her favorite kind of reporting. At the time, there were almost no female correspondents on the front lines of Vietnam.

Wearing a flak jacket, baggy pants, combat boots, and a helmet, Webb was a relentless, intrepid reporter who was unfazed by mortar attacks and enemy fire. She worked her way up to become the Phnom Penh, Cambodia, bureau chief for UPI.

But on April 7, 1971, Webb was captured by a North Vietnamese army unit. Most prisoners were executed, and when a woman similar to Webb was found shot in a shallow grave, the newspapers reported that Webb had died. Her family held a memorial service for her. But after 23 days, Webb was released and made her way out of the

Kate Webb was held captive by North Vietnamese troops for 23 days in 1971.

jungle, suffering from malaria. She nearly died, but she recovered and spent the next 20 years reporting from war zones across Asia.

In 2001, Webb retired because she felt she'd become too old for front-line reporting—the only kind she liked.

Webb died of cancer in 2007 at age 64. Her coolness and courage under pressure showed the world that female war reporters could be just as brave and focused on accuracy as their male colleagues—helping to pave the way for many more women journalists who followed in her footsteps.

Anne Garrels
(1951–)

Born in 1951 in Massachusetts, Anne Garrels went to boarding school in London, England, and then to Radcliffe College in Massachusetts in 1968. She loved all things Russian, and when she took a job at ABC News after college, she found herself flying to the Soviet Union as a correspondent, in part because of her Russian language skills.

The Soviet Union was a totalitarian government, and many Russians were afraid to speak to a reporter. Garrels focused on building trust and relationships with people so that they would feel comfortable speaking freely. She was promoted to bureau chief in Moscow, but her reporting was so effective and disturbing to the Soviet government that she was kicked out of the country in 1982.

Garrels went on to cover conflicts in Nicaragua, El Salvador, Tiananmen Square in China, the Gulf War in Iraq, and the war in Afghanistan. She reported for ABC News, then for NBC News, and later for National Public Radio (NPR).

> *I have found incredibly brave, principled people who risked their lives for the greater good.*
>
> –Anne Garrels

Anne Garrels reported from the roof of a
U.S. marine base in Fallujah, Iraq, 2004.

During the Iraq War, Garrels was one of two female journalists out of 16 journalists taking shelter in a hotel in Baghdad while bombs whistled and exploded around them. At one point all the other journalists had fled, leaving Garrels the only journalist broadcasting from Baghdad. She knew she might be killed or captured at any moment, but she kept reporting.

Garrels has won nearly every major

broadcast award and still continues to write, though she is retired. "I have witnessed more depravity, cruelty, brutality than I ever anticipated or could have imagined possible. But in the midst of this I have found incredibly brave, principled people who risked their lives for the greater good—often ordinary people who, faced with evil, did extraordinary things," she said in a speech for the Connecticut Women's Hall of Fame.

Marie Colvin
(1956–2012)

Legendary war correspondent Marie Colvin began reporting early, writing articles for the *Yale Daily News* as a college student. She studied under the famous journalist and author John Hersey. It was during this time that Colvin decided, "I want to tell the really big stories by telling them through the stories of the individuals, the victims of war." After graduating, Colvin began a lifetime of traveling to some of the most dangerous conflict zones on the planet.

Colvin reported from Libya, where she interviewed dictator Muammar Gaddafi. She reported from the Palestinian territories, where she would sometimes be summoned in the middle of the night for a surprise interview with leader Yasser Arafat. She embedded with Chechen rebels as they fought Russian troops and spent eight days traveling through icy mountain passes to the country of Georgia when the Russians began closing in.

> I want to tell the really big stories by telling them through the stories of the individuals, the victims of war.
>
> —Marie Colvin

In 1999, Colvin sent firsthand reports of the violence coming out of East Timor as that country voted for independence. Most of the other reporters had fled. Her reporting pressured the United Nations into evacuating desperate refugees trapped inside the country.

Colvin was legendarily tough and wisecracking, but the pressure and dangers of her career took their toll. She was a heavy smoker and drinker, and she wore a trademark black eyepatch after being hit in the face with shrapnel and losing an eye in Sri Lanka in 2001. Years of observing brutalities and death affected her. Colvin was haunted by the horrors she had seen and, in 2004, she was diagnosed with post-traumatic stress disorder. But Colvin's passion for reporting wouldn't let her quit.

In 2012, Colvin was covering the Syrian government's siege of the city

Marie Colvin was the first recipient of the Woman of the Year Window to the World Award for her reporting on the war in Sri Lanka.

of Homs. The building she was sheltering in was deliberately shelled. Colvin was killed. In 2019, a United States federal court ruled that the government of Syria should be held responsible for Colvin's death. The courts were sending an important signal—that Syria's targeting of Colvin was a crime and should be treated as such.

Christiane Amanpour
(1958–)

Christiane Amanpour is one of the best-known international correspondents in television and is CNN's chief international anchor. She hosts the news shows *Amanpour* on CNN and *Amanpour & Company* on PBS. Amanpour has reported from war zones all over the world and has won every major broadcast television award.

Born in London in 1958, Amanpour was raised partly in Tehran, Iran. Her mother was English and her father was Iranian. She attended the University of Rhode Island and was hired by a local TV station right out of college. She knew she wanted to work in TV journalism. Specifically, she wanted to be a foreign correspondent. She was hired by CNN and sent to cover the Gulf War, even though she was a junior member of the reporting team. Amanpour's career really took off when she traveled to Bosnia to report on the war taking place in that region. She'd never covered a war in which civilians were targets, and she'd never witnessed genocide. As a journalist, she was determined to remain both objective and moral—a difficult balance, she said in an interview.

Amanpour has reported from Afghanistan, Iran, Pakistan, Somalia, Israel, Rwanda, several countries in Asia, and other conflict zones. In 2004, she was one of very few journalists reporting from the courtroom in which Saddam Hussein was tried. She has interviewed prime ministers, presidents, and royalty. She had the first interview with Jordan's King Abdullah as well as other leaders in the Middle East.

Amanpour uses her profile as one of the world's most famous journalists to campaign for human rights, seeking interviews with education and women's rights activists to draw attention to their causes. In 2007 she was made a CBE, a Commander of the Order of the British Empire—an honor bestowed by the queen. Amanpour is also an honorary citizen of Sarajevo, Bosnia, to recognize her historic reporting there.

Among many other awards, Christiane Amanpour has won two Peabody awards for distinguished achievement in journalism.

Chapter 4

COVERT COMBAT

During the last century, spies have dropped behind enemy lines by parachute, driven motorcycles over mountain passes, and endured harsh interrogations. Some died because of their work. Some gathered information so valuable it changed the course of entire wars—and human history. Stories of spies and secret agents in wartime often seem the stuff of novels. But these women were playing those roles in real life.

Virginia Hall
(1906–1982)

Virginia Hall was born into a wealthy Baltimore family in 1906. She lost a leg in a hunting accident when she was a young woman and, for the rest of her life, used a prosthetic leg she referred to as Cuthbert.

Hall wanted to be an ambassador, but when she applied to the State Department, she encountered heavy prejudice against women. Moreover, the department said,

Virginia Hall, September 1945

the service was only for people without disabilities. Hall was disgusted but undeterred. When World War II began, she volunteered as an ambulance driver for the French army on the front lines. When France fell to the Nazis, Hall fled to England. After a chance meeting with a British secret agent in a train station, she was accepted into the British Special Operations Executive (SOE), England's wartime spy agency.

Hall proved to be one of the most courageous, fierce, and successful spies of the war. She masterminded jailbreaks, organized help for the French Resistance, and managed to dodge the Gestapo when other agents were captured. In 1942, when the Nazis were trying to catch "the Limping Lady," as they called her, she walked for three days in the snow for more than 50 miles (80 kilometers) to escape them.

Hall switched over to the OSS (Office of Strategic Services), the U.S. wartime spy agency. There she became a top leader of French Resistance units. She organized and commanded guerrilla fighting units as they attacked German convoys, liberated villages, and planted bombs.

Hall was awarded the Distinguished Service Cross in 1945, the only U.S. woman to receive that medal. She rarely talked about the war after she came home. Too many of her friends had died talking, she would say. But Hall's spy and guerrilla fighting techniques are still taught and used by CIA agents today. Hall died in 1982 at age 76, the most highly decorated female veteran of World War II.

Christine Granville (Krystyna Skarbek)
(1908–1952)

Christine Granville, who also went by the Polish name Krystyna Skarbek, was one of Britain's most fearless female spies. She was a Jewish countess born in Poland, but her family's fortune collapsed after World War I. When World War II swept through

Europe, Granville went to the SOE office in England and demanded a job as an agent.

Granville proved to be a calm, ruthless spy who once bit her own tongue during a Nazi interrogation to make it look as though she was coughing up blood. The interrogators thought she had the deadly, contagious disease tuberculosis and released her.

Granville famously obtained microfilm with Nazi plans to invade the Soviet Union, a British ally. She skied out of Poland with the information hidden in the lining of her leather gloves. It went straight to British Prime Minister Winston Churchill and changed the course of the war.

In 1944, she was dropped by parachute behind enemy lines in France. The average lifespan of an agent in Nazi-occupied France was six weeks. Granville not only survived, she also single-handedly convinced an entire detachment of Polish soldiers fighting for the Germans to defect. When two of her fellow agents were being

Christine Granville (shown at age 19) was the longest-serving of Britain's wartime female agents.

held by the Gestapo and were within hours of their execution, Granville rode a bicycle 25 miles (40 km) to the camp where

CHRISTINE GRANVILLE'S SPY GEAR

Christine Granville used a variety of spy equipment that seems lifted from the pages of a James Bond novel. She would embed valuable microfilm in bars of soap and conceal bomb detonators within the middle of hard candy balls. She and her fellow agents would test the rate at which the candies dissolved in a school swimming pool. Some write that Granville carried a compass hidden behind a hair clip and a cigarette with a magnifying glass concealed at the tip. She also had a commando knife, a flashlight, and a cyanide tablet sewn into her skirt hem. She never needed the tablet, but if she had ever been caught and tortured, Granville could have used it to take her own life.

Cameras like this could be sewn into a coat, with only the button lens exposed.

they were being held. There, she told a head officer that the French Resistance knew about the captured agents and had arranged for him, the head officer, to be killed if he did not release them. She was so convincing that the officer let the agents go.

Granville was heavily decorated for bravery, but the British government dismissed her from service after the war. Her spy work over, she took a low-wage job at a hotel. Then tragedy struck: At age 44, Granville was stabbed by a man she worked with at the hotel. She had survived the Gestapo and years of dangerous spying only to die in a brutal personal assault.

Marie-Madeleine Fourcade
(1909–1989)

Marie-Madeleine Fourcade's code name was "Hedgehog." Born in France but raised in Shanghai, she was the educated daughter of a prosperous steamship company executive. She certainly never anticipated

Marie-Madeleine Fourcade, code-named Hedgehog, provided crucial information to the Allies as a leader in the French Resistance.

she would become a spymaster and major leader of the French Resistance in World War II.

In 1939, when the war broke out, Fourcade was living in France near the

Pyrenees Mountains. She quickly joined the French Resistance, the clandestine group of freedom fighters working to resist Nazi occupation of their country. Fourcade helped leaders organize what would be called the Alliance network, or Noah's Ark, named because the agents each had an animal code name. The Alliance transmitted secret information about Nazi movements to Allied commanders in Britain. When the leader, Georges Loustaunau-Lacau, was arrested, Fourcade began running the unit and directing agents.

The unit gathered information about German military hardware and movements of submarines and sent it to England. The crucial information Fourcade was able to provide was so helpful that England sent over a wireless radio operator to assist her.

But the operator they sent was a double agent—a British spy who was also spying for Germany. The operator reported Fourcade to the Gestapo, and Fourcade was arrested in 1942. She managed to escape and went into hiding, eventually surviving four arrests by the Nazis. Each time, she escaped or was released. Once, she was smuggled out of France in a mailbag to avoid detection. As many spies did, Fourcade carried cyanide pills to take her own life in case she was caught and tortured by the Nazis.

But Fourcade survived. She had provided essential information to aid the Allied cause during her service. She went on to live a long life and died in Paris at age 79.

Nancy Wake
(1912–2011)

Nancy Wake was a New Zealand–born spy and covert fighter during World War II. She spied for England and was so good at escaping detection that the Germans called her "the White Mouse."

Wake was born in New Zealand and raised in Sydney, Australia. While working as a nurse in Berlin and Vienna during the

1930s, Wake was disgusted by the violent anti-Semitism, or prejudice against Jewish people, that she observed. She vowed to fight the Nazis. She married wealthy industrialist Henri Fiocca, and together they moved to France to join the French Resistance in 1940.

The Resistance was the underground movement of Allied freedom fighters who resisted the Nazis during the time that France was occupied by Germany. Wake hid fighters fleeing Nazis in her home and then would escort them across the Pyrenees Mountains to safety in Spain.

Wake grew into a resistance leader, organizing hundreds of fighters ahead of the planned Allied D-Day invasion at Normandy. Trained by England's spy operation, the SOE, Wake was dropped by parachute behind enemy lines in France. There, she received nighttime parachute drops of supplies and set up communication lines. At one point, when the communication lines were severed,

Nancy Wake supported the Allies as a spy and guerilla fighter for the Resistance.

she rode a bicycle 124 miles (200 km) through enemy territory to deliver essential messages.

Wake was a guerrilla fighter as well. She was trained in hand-to-hand combat and once killed a German guard at a factory by karate-chopping the back of his neck.

The Germans put a bounty on Wake, offering payment to have her killed. She made an incredible escape to Spain on the back of a coal truck after jumping from a slow-moving train while Germans fired at her.

Historians estimate that Wake saved hundreds of lives during the war. She survived her time as a spy and became a decorated hero of the French Resistance and the Allied operation. She died in London at age 98.

Noor Inayat Khan
(1914–1944)

Noor Inayat Khan's code name was "Madeleine." She was many things—a descendent of Indian royalty, the child of Indian intellectuals, an educated woman who went to college at the Sorbonne in Paris, and a spy.

After her death, Noor Inayat Khan was awarded Britain's George Cross for her acts of heroism.

Khan was born to a wealthy Indian family in Moscow in 1914. They were living in England when World War II began. Khan felt a need to help the war operation but in a way that did not involve killing, which went against her Sufi faith.

She joined Britain's intelligence operation, the SOE. She was trained as a secret agent and radio operator. In June 1943, Khan was dropped behind enemy lines in France, carrying heavy radio equipment and tasked with setting up communication between England and the French Resistance fighters.

The work was incredibly dangerous, and agents were often killed after only weeks in the field. Khan managed to continue her work for several months. But in October 1943, a French woman betrayed Khan to the Gestapo. Khan was arrested. Because she had kept copies of her secret radio signals, the Nazis used those to trick Britain into sending new agents over, where they were immediately captured by the enemy.

Khan was sent to a Gestapo prison. There, she was chained, kept in solitary confinement, and tortured. She managed to escape for a few hours but was recaptured and sent to the Dachau concentration camp in Germany. On September 13, 1944, she was executed by the Nazis along with three other women spies. It was reported that her last word was "*Liberté.*" Freedom.

The fighters of the French Resistance played a major role in the D-Day Allied invasions at Normandy, France. They distracted and harassed German troops and blew up key railroads and bridges the Nazis needed to access.

Timeline

1914 In August, Edith Cavell begins smuggling wounded Allied soldiers to safety in the Netherlands.

1915 Flora Murray sets up the Endell Street Military Hospital, a hospital run entirely by women.

1916 Along with her husband, Alice Askew publishes a book of her war correspondence and thoughts entitled *The Stricken Land: Serbia as We Saw It.*

1917 The Russian government creates the Russian Women's Battalion of Death and appoints Maria Bochkareva as commander.

1937 Martha Gellhorn arrives in Spain to cover the Spanish Civil War for *Collier's* magazine, carrying a backpack and $50.

1939 Clare Hollingworth breaks the news of the German invasion of Poland, signaling the start of World War II.

1940 Nancy Wake joins the French Resistance at the start of World War II.

1942 Susan Travers drives through enemy lines surrounding her camp in the Libyan desert, paving the way for other Allied troops to follow.

1942 Virginia Hall, working as a secret agent for Britain, walks 50 miles (80 km) over three days, in the snow, to elude capture by the Gestapo.

1943 Noor Inayat Khan is dropped behind enemy lines in France in order to set up lines of communication between England and the French Resistance fighters.

1944 Charity Adams Earley becomes leader of the first all–African American, all-women unit of soldiers to be deployed overseas.

1945 Jane Kendeigh becomes the first nurse to provide care on an active Pacific battlefield during World War II when she lands on Iwo Jima on March 6.

1954 Geneviève de Galard receives France's highest military honor when she becomes a knight in the French Foreign Legion on April 29 after tending to the wounded at Dien Bien Phu.

1970 Gloria Emerson arrives in Vietnam to report on the Vietnam War, one of the few female correspondents on the ground.

1971 While reporting for the UPI, Kate Webb is captured and held in the Vietnamese jungle by a North Vietnamese fighting unit.

2003 Linda McTague becomes the first woman to command a fighter squadron in the U.S. Air Force.

2004 Leigh Ann Hester defends her squad against enemy fire in Iraq and survives a 45-minute firefight with extraordinary bravery, protecting the lives of her fellow soldiers.

2008 Monica Lin Brown receives the Silver Star for valor after rescuing fellow soldiers in Afghanistan the year before.

2012 Marie Colvin is killed in a targeted attack by the Syrian government while reporting from the city of Homs.

Glossary

Allies—those countries allied in opposition to the Central Powers (Germany, Austria-Hungary, and Turkey) in World War I or to the Axis powers (Germany, Italy, and Japan) in World War II

Blitz—a German aerial bombing campaign against the United Kingdom in 1940 and 1941

clandestine—secretive

commandeer—to compel to perform military service

decimate—to destroy or seriously damage

defect—to give up loyalty to a country or cause and leave it

elite—a select, superior group

embed—to attach a journalist to a military unit for the purpose of covering a conflict

evacuation—the act of removing people from a place of danger to a safer place

execute—to carry out a death sentence on a person ordered to die by law

genocide—organized killing of an entire cultural or political group

Gestapo—the secret police of Nazi Germany

guerrilla—a type of military action using small groups of fighters to carry out surprise attacks against enemy forces

hallucinate—to see or hear things that are not real

martyr—a person who gives their life for a worthy cause

militant—aggressively active or combative

prohibition—the forbidding of something by law

racism—prejudice and discrimination against a group or a person because of their race

suffragist—a person who works for voting rights, especially voting rights for women

Sufi—a religion that incorporates Islamic mysticism

underground—concealed and done in secret

Critical Thinking Questions

1. The women in this book faced many challenges. What particular challenge stood out most to you? Describe the challenge and how the woman was able to overcome it.
2. Historically, women in the military have had restricted roles. For instance, for most of history, women could not fight in combat. Do you agree or disagree with restricting the role of women in the military? Explain your position.
3. Women in war often risked their lives to help others, report honestly, or carry out their assigned mission. Have you ever been asked to make a personal sacrifice or do something out of the ordinary? If so, describe what happened and your feelings about it.

Further Reading

O'Brien, Keith. *Fly Girls Young Readers' Edition: How Five Daring Women Defied All Odds and Made Aviation History.* Boston: Houghton Mifflin Harcourt, 2019.

Ross, Ailsa. *The Girl Who Rode a Shark & Other Stories of Daring Women.* Ontario, Canada: Pajama Press, 2019.

Stanborough, Rebecca J. *25 Women Who Ruled.* North Mankato, MN: Capstone Press, 2018.

Internet Sites

History At a Glance: Women in World War II
The National WWII Museum
https://www.nationalww2museum.org/students-teachers/student-resources/research-starters/women-wwii

National Women's History Museum
https://www.womenshistory.org/

The Women's Memorial
https://www.womensmemorial.org/

Source Notes

p. 4, "I have had the opportunity…" C. Todd Lopez, "First Female Four-Star General Retires from Army," U.S. Army, August 15, 2012, https://www.army.mil/article/85606/first_female_four_star_general_retires_from_army

p. 8, "I realize that patriotism…" "Edith Cavell," The National World War I Museum and Memorial, Nd, https://www.theworldwar.org/learn/edith-cavell

p. 13, "Her service to her comrades…" "Citation Accompanying the Medal of Freedom Presented to Genevieve de Galard-Terraube," The American Presidency Project, July 29, 1954, https://www.presidency.ucsb.edu/documents/citation-accompanying-the-medal-freedom-presented-genevieve-de-galard-terraube

p. 14, "Medicine is one of those places…" Meghann Myers, "The Army's First Black, Female 3-Star Was Inspired to Serve by Her Father—and Star Trek," *Army Times,* February 27, 2017, https://www.armytimes.com/news/your-army/2017/02/27/the-army-s-first-black-female-3-star-was-inspired-to-serve-by-her-father-and-star-trek/

p. 17, "[Brown's] bravery, unselfish actions and medical aid…" Associated Press, "Female Medic Earns Silver Star in Afghan War," *NBC News,* updated March 9, 2008, http://www.nbcnews.com/id/23547346/ns/us_news-military/t/female-medic-earns-silver-star-afghan-war/#.XbCQk9UpDIU

p. 21, "I just happen to be a person…" Alan Riding, "A Legionnaire, She Was Never Timid in Amour or War," *New York Times,* April 21, 2001, https://www.nytimes.com/2001/04/21/books/a-legionnaire-she-was-never-timid-in-amour-or-war.html

p. 23, "Over my dead body, sir." Richard Goldstein, "Charity Adams Earley, Black Pioneer in Wacs, Dies at 83," *New York Times,* January 22, 2002, https://www.nytimes.com/2002/01/22/us/charity-adams-earley-black-pioneer-in-wacs-dies-at-83.html

p. 25, "not settle for being…" Bob Haskell, "ANG Commander Does Not See Herself as Pioneer," U.S. Air Force, March 19, 2004, https://www.af.mil/News/Article-Display/Article/137357/ang-commander-does-not-see-herself-as-pioneer/

p. 28, "right beside" Michael Biesecker, "First Woman to Lead GIs in Combat—and Look at the Thanks She Got," *Seattle Times,* January 25, 2013, https://www.seattletimes.com/nation-world/first-woman-to-lead-gis-in-combat-8212-and-look-at-the-thanks-she-got/

p. 29, "I was trained to do…" Rachel Martin, "Silver Star Recipient A Reluctant Hero," NPR Morning Edition, February 22, 2011, https://www.npr.org/2011/02/22/133847765/silver-star-recipient-a-reluctant-hero

p. 32, "…words could hardly give…" Alice and Claude Askew, "Full Text of *The Stricken Land: Serbia as We Saw It,*" Internet Archive, Nd, https://archive.org/stream/strickenlandserb00aske/strickenlandserb00aske_djvu.txt

p. 33, "You go into a hospital…" Rick Lyman, "Martha Gellhorn, Daring Writer, Dies at 89," *New York Times,* February 17, 1998, https://www.nytimes.com/1998/02/17/arts/martha-gellhorn-daring-writer-dies-at-89.html

p. 42, "I have witnessed more depravity…" "Anne Garrels," Connecticut Women's Hall of Fame, Nd, https://www.cwhf.org/inductees/anne-garrels

p. 42, "I want to tell the really big…" Lulu Garcia-Navarro, "A New Biography of Marie Colvin, Eyewitness to War," NPR Weekend Edition Sunday, November 4, 2018, https://www.npr.org/2018/11/04/663571722/a-new-biography-of-marie-colvin-eyewitness-to-war

All internet sites were accessed on April 8, 2020.

Select Bibliography

Bernstein, Adam, "Nancy Wake, 'White Mouse' of World War II, Dies at 98," *Washington Post,* August 9, 2011, https://www.washingtonpost.com/local/obituaries/nancy-wake-white-mouse-of-world-war-ii-dies-at-98/2011/08/08/gIQABvPT5I_story.html Accessed on February 23, 2020.

"Christiane Amanpour," Biography, September 26, 2019, https://www.biography.com/media-figure/christiane-amanpour Accessed on February 23, 2020.

Clifton, Tony, "Kate Webb," *The Guardian*, May 15, 2007, https://www.theguardian.com/media/2007/may/15/guardianobituaries.pressandpublishing Accessed on February 23, 2020.

Fox, Margalit, "Clare Hollingworth, Reporter Who Broke News of World War II, Dies at 105," *New York Times*, January 10, 2017, https://www.nytimes.com/2017/01/10/business/media/clare-hollingworth-reporter-who-broke-news-of-world-war-ii-dies-at-105.html Accessed on February 23, 2020.

Goldstein, Richard, "Charity Adams Earley, Black Pioneer in Wacs, Dies at 83," *New York Times*, January 22, 2002, https://www.nytimes.com/2002/01/22/us/charity-adams-earley-black-pioneer-in-wacs-dies-at-83.html Accessed on November 11, 2019.

Goodridge, Elisabeth, "Overlooked No More: Maria Bochkareva, Who Led Women into Battle in WWI," *New York Times*, April 25, 2018, https://www.nytimes.com/2018/04/25/obituaries/overlooked-maria-bochkareva.html Accessed on February 23, 2020.

Held, Jenny and Don K. Nakayama, "Louisa Garrett Anderson and Flora Murray: Redefining Gender Roles in Military Medicine," *Bulletin of the American College of Surgeons*, April 1, 2019, http://bulletin.facs.org/2019/04/louisa-garrett-anderson-and-flora-murray-redefining-gender-roles-in-military-medicine/ Accessed February 23, 2020.

Lyman, Rick, "Martha Gellhorn, Daring Writer, Dies at 89," *New York Times,* February 17, 1998, https://www.nytimes.com/1998/02/17/arts/martha-gellhorn-daring-writer-dies-at-89.html Accessed on November 11, 2019.

Martin, Rachel, "Silver Star Recipient A Reluctant Hero," NPR Morning Edition, February 22, 2011, https://www.npr.org/2011/02/22/133847765/silver-star-recipient-a-reluctant-hero Accessed on November 11, 2019.

Riding, Alan, "A Legionnaire, She Was Never Timid in Amour or War," *New York Times*, April 21, 2001, https://www.nytimes.com/2001/04/21/books/a-legionnaire-she-was-never-timid-in-amour-or-war.html Accessed on November 11, 2019.

Tsang, Amie, "Overlooked No More: Noor Inayat Khan, Indian Princess and British Spy," *New York Times,* November 28, 2018, https://www.nytimes.com/2018/11/28/obituaries/noor-inayat-khan-overlooked.html Accessed on February 23, 2020.

Zabecki, David T., "This Woman Was the Angel of Dien Bien Phu," HistoryNet, December 2018, https://www.historynet.com/valor-genevieve-de-galard.htm Accessed on February 23, 2020.

About the Author

Emma Carlson Berne is the author of many books of historical nonfiction and biography for children and young adults. She lives in Cincinnati with her husband and three little boys.

Index